Penned In

by

Karen Mooney & Gaynor Kane

First published 2020 by The Hedgehog Poetry Press,

5 Coppack House, Churchill Avenue, Clevedon. BS21 6QW

www.hedgehogpress.co.uk

Copyright © Karen Mooney & Gaynor Kane 2020

The right of Karen Mooney & Gaynor Kane to be identified as the authors of this work has been asserted in accordance with the Copyright, Designs and Patents Act 1988. All rights reserved. No part of this publication may be reproduced, stored in or introduced into a retrieval system, or transmitted in any form, or by any means (electronic, mechanical, photocopying, recording or otherwise) without prior written permissions of the publisher. Any person who does any unauthorised act in relation to this publication may be liable for criminal prosecution and civil claims for damages.

ISBN: 978-1-913499-54-9

These poems are for you, for all of you.

They were written during the pandemic, mostly in the early months when we all became acutely aware of the heroes around us who bravely went about the business of saving lives as we stayed at home to do the same.

Those everyday heroes who went to work, ensuring the continuance of essential services and the volunteers who gave of their time and skills to support others.

Those who have endured pain, worry or anxiety through suffering and loss, perhaps even waiting on treatment for other health conditions. You too are heroes, as are those who struggle with their mental health just to get through each day.

We have all struggled to find ways to connect throughout this period, and we hope that these poems will contribute towards the many conversations around these unprecedented circumstances.

Gaynor & Karen

Contents

Penned In	7
View from my Window	8
We're all in this together?	9
Bridge:	10
Applause	11
Learning BSL during lockdown, April 2020	12
Stilling the World	13
Puppets	15
Shielding	16
Another Sunrise	17
Baby's Breath	18
Evening Oranges, East Belfast, July 2020	19
Shepherding	20
The Butterfly Effect	21
"I Touched You"	22

Penned In

As free-rangers, we often hide
in plain sight even from ourselves.
Cooped up, confronted by
a wilderness of mirrors,
despite the illusion of space,
we're pushing back the walls.

Thoughts, like birds, wings clipped,
are grounded. They flap, fox fear
quivering, launching at their cage.
Some break for freedom, scratching
the surface, unable to fly, off the lay.
Slurred by the spirit of confusion,
unable to form a sentence whilst
they're serving one.

They graze, pecking at one
source of enrichment after another.
Dust covers cool in the heat
till a welcome sun kills the mites
that make them itch and scratch.

Nature takes her course.
The plumage will recover,
tail feathers shaking,
all flocked up, a clutch of words
will soon appear.

View from my Window

Is a Facebook group with over 2 million members. A window on the world during a global pandemic. As people are told to #stayhome #savelives a simple scroll can take you on a virtual spin around Earth. From Qatar to Queensland, New York to the Netherlands, Haiti to Honolulu, Belfast to Bristol.

she scrolled down, wondering
about their backstory; speculating
about their secrets.

Last night he told her he was going to put her out through the window. The Naked Wine delivery arrived before lunch and by 4 o'clock he had reviewed the Pinot and Malbec. He reminisced about their last holiday to the Spanish Vineyard whilst she rubbed the elbow that had felt the impact of the villa's tiled floor. Suffering insomnia, she spent much of the darkest hours standing looking out the large picture window of their living room.

following the slow movement
of moon shadows, never looking straight
into her ghostly reflection.

This morning, the view from her window was worthy of posting in the Facebook group. Her garden was in dappled sunlight, dew dropped leaves sparkled and bright pink rhododendrons were buzzing with bees. The small wooded area across the street had a jay bird visiting. She watched it fly from branch to branch, thinking how beautiful its dusky pink body and blue tipped wings were. Glancing at her backpack, she put on a cardigan to cover up the pink and blue patches on her arms. She was just waiting for him to doze off for his post fry-up snooze and then she was going out through the door and down the road to the phone box. She squiggled down the number of the helpline,

gripped the piece of paper
in her hand and pulled up the
zipper on her coat.

We're all in this together?

Same storm, same boat.
Accommodation - first class,
lifeboats, entertainment
on upper decks with space,
pools and views.

Served with distinction
by those who step up
from lower decks, working
their passage on this titanic
journey; returning below
to jostle for space.

Don't they know their place?

Herded into cabins, fevers
rise, spreading tension,
fuelling dissention,
a need to escape,

so,

they take a chance,

happenstance.

We're all in this together...

Bridge:

> a construction spanning a divide, supporting the ends;
> an arch;
> a connection

for Michael, 26th April 2020

Twenty-one years ago
we stood on the edge
of Devil's Bridge, on the edge
of the Atlantic, at the edge
of Antigua with nothing
between there and Europe
except enormity of marriage and sea.

The rocks, the vast ocean,
in iron grey, dark blue and violet tones of iolite.
Water sapphire, gemstone which symbolises
our time together,
the *Viking's compass*,
they first used slivers as polarising filters
to navigate the seas.

We stood, still, hand in hand.
listening to crashing waves
on the underside of the arch;
watching water whistle through blowholes,
we felt salt on our skin.

Hand in hand, we'd made a pact,
we knew we were jumping
off the edge together, into a life where
everything would be alright if we just held
each other, if we just held
each other's hand.

Applause

Resounding up and down
the country, a polite ripple
swells to tension fuelled
ovations demanding an encore.

Fingered cymbals pound
out a frenzied timbre of gratitude,
vibrating in a momentum
that mandates principals
long after the performance.

Afterwards,

we breathe out
silent hope packed prayers,
channel hop to news that drowns
spontaneous acts with honk laden,
atonal governmental noise.

Learning BSL during lockdown, April 2020

For Michael Wilson

Last night in a Zoom room
I learned to finger spell in BSL,
the first part of the alphabet up to M
but we got N as a bonus
and O and U as we pointed out the five-digit vowels.

You taught us good,
good morning, good afternoon,
good evening and good night.
We gave ourselves jazz-hand applause.

G is like one-potato-two-potato
or a knuckle column of the Giants Causeway
and G exploding outward is gold
add swimming, slithering,
fingers forward, for fish.

The longest word I can fingerspell
is f - i - d - d - l - e - d - e - e - d - e - e
but it takes me an eternity.

Now I can spell out b-e-a-c-h.
It ends with a swift single rub
to remove all the invisible grains of sand
off the palm of my hand.

Next week, I will be able spell out c-o-a-s-t
but I will not be allowed to go there.

Stilling the World

Wash those hands. Behind the ears?
Yes, those too, might just ease fears.
That's if you can still get soap,
we're beyond hope with hoarders,
no fears of borders just gather in,
that's no sin, love thy neighbour,
well...after yourself. If its left on the shelf
you can have some too, sure,
don't we all use the loo? And the hands
must be clean, you know where they've been!

Lets' get some perspective, or even some distance.

Let's talk from six feet away. What's that you say?
No - email, it's safer, wireless, hopefully this bloody virus
is not online. But what if it is? No Facebook, Twitter,
LinkedIn, Snapchat, Reddit, Instagram. You're not a fan?
Where have you been? Outdoors? Not just posting pics
of the last place you went, your dinner, outfit, selfie,
with all good intent. Sure, they'll pop up as memories
or bloody incendiaries, firing you up about freedoms lost.

But think of the cost if you don't stay home.
You're not alone, we're in this together,
won't be forever but some will never...

We won't go there, but we do have to think
about others and how we're on the brink,
on a ledge – it's taken a pandemic
to make us pledge to help each other.

The old, the sick, the homeless, all,
as we hear the clock tick, time −
passing through our hands as we
lose our grip on what we held dear.

Reassessing priorities - holding loved ones near,
in mind, think kind.

And all around, heroes
emerge, stepping up as we're stood down,
facing invisible enemy in mask and gown.
Ill equipped, hiding fears, self-isolating from
loved ones, to protect us − on brink of tears.
Alone with thoughts whilst we stay home
and wait and pray, if you want, some can't,
faith contracted but there's always hope
as life goes on.

Nature's story, unredacted
blossoms and seeds on the world's page.
A composition, set to a sound that we now hear

As we lay quiet, she awakens in our ear to trill
a lesson in time: cherish each moment, be still.

Puppets

after Jerzy Kędziora, a Polish Sculptor

A puppet on a string,
frozen in form,
unable to dance,
or kick my bent leg out,
wave with my straight arm
or smile with my featureless face
because my master
is a statue.
A sculpture balancing on a wire
forever crouching over me,
dangling me above
the gawping open-mouthed tourists
who cannot hear me laugh
when the seagull shits on their heads.

Now, the streets are bare,
save the baby bear
who has wakened early from hibernation,
a herd of deer
in socially distanced single-file formation
and one masked human
capturing the sight
for his social media marionettes.

Shielding

our fine bone china
collects dust with the crystal
defining moments
locked away for safekeeping
brought out for celebration

Another Sunrise

On social media platforms they call for polycotton; curtains & duvet covers and stitchers & sewers to make scrubs. The brighter the better, so that those in ICU can see the colours of the rainbow and have hope.

* * *

Getting dressed for work, she pulls on the bottoms with their wide legs and elastic waist. They are stitched together with squares, a patchwork of kind peoples' quilts. Sunshine yellow, leaf green and sky blue. Taking the colours of nature with her, she walks into the ward. She has pinned a picture of her smiling face onto the plastic apron over her multicoloured tunic top so that her coughing patients can see what was hidden under the mask and spit screen. She explains to those still conscious that she is smiling and uses signs for okay and good. Especially for the older patients who would like to read her lips. Above her ponytail is a crocheted rainbow strip with wooden buttons at either end, attached to this is the elastic of her mask. It has brought so much relief as her ears had been rubbed raw. She listens to the beeps and whirrs of machines and finishes writing up her end-of-shift notes. Every inch of her is exhausted.

Earlier that week, she watched out the window as her neighbour and her children delivered her ear saver. Along with a disinfected care package of custard creams, dark chocolate, a vanilla sponge decorated with sprinkles and several paintings of rainbows and hearts. The children waved and her friend clapped. When they left, she slid down the wall, curled up into a ball and wept.

* * *

Just before dawn, she pushes the hospital bed down the long white corridor, into the lift, along another corridor lined with Frida Kahlo inspired artwork, past the shop and café, out to the carpark. Aligning the bed so that the horizon is visible between the two high-rise buildings, she puts the brakes on, plumps pillows and props Robert up, making him as comfortable as possible. They hear the morning masses of birds singing a requiem. She moves two metres behind the bed, lifts her face shield, removes her mask and they watch his last sunrise, together.

Baby's Breath

*For Fergus Orson James Adams, born 29 May, 2020
and his grandparents, Jim and Julia Adams.*

Your tiny leaf-like fingers unfurl
as we trill news of your arrival.
Hope fills the air as you exhale
heralding the future.

Long stems stand proud,
heads lifted heavenward
as you breathe life
into a fading bouquet.

Sharing the same soil, we'll toil
to tend your roots, watch you
spread each year then bloom,
cast your seed on a waft of joy
to settle in loam of your own.

Evening Oranges, East Belfast, July 2020

layered sky:
sherbert laces
tangerine segments
papaya and cantaloupe slices
coral clouds

royal visits:
monarch, admiral and viceroys
resting on lichen crusted sandstone walls
under flags with williamite stars

loyal landscape:
honeysuckle and tea rose cross-stitching a hedge
peach pie cooling on a windowsill
under amber glass
garden lillies, tiger and fire, forest flames, red hot pokers
californian poppies, crocosmia, and cosmos

sunset supper on garden swing seat:
golden shred
on hot
buttered
toast

Shepherding

If they're not rounded up
how will I count them?
Each time I begin, they scatter;
one way, then the other.

Dispersed amongst the plumped-up
hillocks on which I rest my head;
they graze on my conscience,
gorge on the roots of the past,
nibble at new growth;
fertilising my acres of doubt.

I watch, pleading with the wise counsellor
passing by, staring at his moon-shaped face.
His slow-moving hands urge calm;
I breathe slowly,
trying to match
his steady heartbeat.

Recalling that old shepherd's saying that:
Sheep obey no man
they obey the stars.
I surrender to the night.

The Butterfly Effect

Tomorrow,
for the first time in four months,
I am allowed to see   my parents inside,
in their natural habitat   of the care home.
They have been well cocooned,   the doors firmly closed
to keep
the invisible threat at bay.
I picture them   swaddled
in sleeping bags   suspended   from the ceiling light,
human caterpillars
becoming covid-free
butterflies.

I have been told
to wear a surgical mask   and wash my hands
in the porch   for the length of time   it takes me to sing
happy birthday.
If I see them together,   I can stay for 20 minutes
but if I visit them in their separate rooms
I can have 15 minutes   with each.
Ironic   how the breeze of a bat's wing
can create a terrible
tempest.

"I Touched You"

For Bill

It was spoken like a confession
as if seeking absolution
for breaking the rules of social distance,
just one instance.

Emerging from lockdown
for a socially distanced coffee, a full embrace
would have bookended our meeting
but this new normal required different social graces.

Contact, like water trembling
around this huge boulder
of fear that we all now shoulder,
longing its touch yet missing it so, so much
we dam our flow, building defences
that defy our own senses.

Dispensing with hugs
to show how much we care,
dispatching kisses into thin air,
wrapping arms around ourselves.
We're compelled to express the unspoken
amidst everything that's broken
to offer a token of what would normally
be pressed on skin.

Quite a task, through a mask
and steamed up glasses,
amidst the masses of signals
that we no longer transmit or receive
and yet we still believe in communing,
still fine tuning how we intermingle.
Tricky if we're single seeking a mate, partner, friend –
just how do you tell and tend
those gentle expressions of love?

I search for clues in my companion.
Stance, bearing, are the shoulders defeated
like snow boughed branches
or open to perching happenstances?
The eyes, like doors welcome me in
and the cheeks plumped like pillows feathered with grins.
The voice, indulgent with words that could cushion a fall,
full and mellow with the warmth of a shawl.

All this I feel, without having to trace
the wrapping of kindness, the skin on his face.
And yet, I too, feel myself reach from within
but I brake my intent, lest I place risk on him.
We part, and I internalise my concern
that his yearn for touch may leave him more susceptible
to the unacceptable - which to him is isolation.

Yes, yes, you really touched me.

Acknowledgements

We gratefully acknowledge the following publications and platforms in which these poems first appeared: *Cupid's Arrow Poems of Love* (Hedgehog Poetry Press, 2020), EastSide Arts Festival, Island Arts Centre, NVTV (Northern Visions Television) and Pendemic.ie

Special thanks to family and friends. Also, Mark Davidson, Editor of the Hedgehog Poetry Press, for the opportunity to have these poems published and for his ongoing support and encouragement.

Karen's poetry has been published in the USA, UK and Ireland. Her work first appeared with Hedgehog Poetry Press in *The Road to Clevedon Pier* and she has two further publications with them in the pipeline.

Follow her on Twitter @1karenmooney or Facebook @observationsbykaren

Gaynor has two poetry pamphlets and a full collection, all published by the Hedgehog Poetry Press; they are *Circling the Sun*, *Memory Forest* and *Venus in Pink Marble* (2018, 2019 and 2020 respectively).

Follow her on Twitter @gaynorkane or read more at www.gaynorkane.com.

www.ingramcontent.com/pod-product-compliance
Lightning Source LLC
Chambersburg PA
CBHW021455080526
44588CB00009B/863